Elephant Rush Hour

Thoughts and Prayers

Jenny Hawke

To Katy, who showed me the love of God,
and taught me to pursue him with all my heart.

First Published 2012
Text and artwork Jenny Hawke

Published, edited and distributed by TLM Trading Limited
www.tlmtrading.com

Books by Eddie Askew and Jenny Hawke
Walking into the Light (with Stephanie Bell), *Making a Mark, There was a Garden*

Jenny Hawke has asserted her right to be identified as the author of this work in
accordance with the Copyright, Designs and Patents Act, 1988.

All rights and subsidiary rights have been granted to
The Leprosy Mission Trading Limited.

Design and production by Creative Plus Publishing Ltd,
www.creative-plus.co.uk

Printed and bound in Singapore by Imago

ISBN 978-0-902731-98-1

Cover picture: The Taj Mahal by Jenny Hawke

Foreword

As a child growing up in India, I didn't spend much time thinking of the past or the future. I was far too busy and happy in the present, exploring the paddy fields nearby, looking for frogs in the small pond or playing with other missionary kids. Dad and Mum were working with The Leprosy Mission and our home was a place called Purulia in West Bengal. Our childhood, as I now realise, was an unusual one, and a very happy one.

As we get older, we're more likely to look back at our experiences, and hopefully learn from them. Some of the thoughts in this book have come from my childhood and it has been interesting seeing those times from a different perspective and recognising God's presence in them. I like 'thought for the day' books, as I often feel the need to focus my mind before the start of the day, to remember the larger purposes of life, and to remind myself that God is with me right here, right now, on my journey through life.

So today, read on and take it slowly, savouring your reactions as they come to you. Turn the thought over, look at it from another angle, take another bite… This journey, in which we hope to know God more day by day, is to my joy, also a journey during which I am learning to love myself, and to revel in who I am, and who I might grow to be.

Remember, there is only one of me, and only one of you. 'Precious in His sight', and our names are written on the palm of His hand.

Jenny Hawke

J. Hawke.

Elephants in the rush hour

Zephaniah 3:17
With his love, he will calm all your fears. He will rejoice over you with joyful songs.
(*New Living Translation*)

We were in Jaipur, in the north of India, about to visit the beautiful Red Palace on the top of a rocky plateau. The transport on offer was on the back of an elephant. Initially, I thought, 'Great!', but the closer I got, the more my courage failed me. The top of the elephant looked a long way up, so I decided to walk up the road myself. What I hadn't understood was that there was only one road up, which meant I was sharing the track with all the elephants, going up and going down, and it was very narrow. As I began, I found myself in the strange position of being incredibly close to the rear of one elephant while having the trunk and tusks of another within twelve inches of my rear.

To make matters worse, I then saw another elephant coming down the hill towards me on the right. How many elephants can you squeeze onto one road at the same time? The answer is, a lot. A local woman, in full Rajasthani costume, noticed the expression on my face, took my hand and walked up the road with me, smiling her reassurance. This was something she did every day.

How strange. I face the horribly busy rush-hour traffic where I live on a daily basis without thinking about it, and for her, this was her rush-hour. The difference being, hers was full of elephants, and mine, cars. She would probably have felt just as worried if she was facing the traffic on my high street for the first time.

Seven thousand miles of difference between us, but we both experience the rush hour, and looking at the smell and the mess that both can produce, I know which I prefer. It has to be the elephants.

Lord,
the world is a wonderful place,
taking me out of my comfort zone
and giving me a new perspective.
And wherever I go,
you are there.
Walking in the dust
or driving on unforgiving tarmac,
you are there,
waiting for me to walk with you.
Let me hold your hand today.

Saving face

Proverbs 16:18
First pride, then the crash – the bigger the ego, the harder the fall.
(*The Message*)

Jessie, our daughter, has always been a fast runner, winning races with ease and a smile on her face. Once she missed the starter's gun and still managed to win even though she started several yards behind.

We have a long garden and used to set up a race circuit for Jessie and Sam when they were young. On this occasion, I think Jessie was four and Sam was six. We have it on video, the start of the race, with Sam momentarily ahead as Jessie began to speed up. The next four circuits show Jessie ahead and Sam lagging behind, that is until he fell over. The race was over and he looked relieved. Jessie was, as usual, triumphant.

Years later, we watched the video again, and there it was, the distress on his face because Jessie was winning, followed by an obvious pause for thought and a very deliberate fall to save his bruised pride. He had been found out. We laughed, especially Sam, because it looked so obvious with hindsight.

Pride is strong in all of us. We want to be seen as doing well, wanting to win, some of us more than others, and when we're not we look for a way out, an excuse. Learning to look at ourselves honestly with loving acceptance is something we all need, and God's unconditional love for us, through Jesus, is the best example of all. For, if God is for us, who are we to argue with him?

Lord,
my pride is a funny thing,
and I can get defensive
when I sense criticism coming my way.
Looking for a way out,
so I won't look small.
But, when I take a step back,
I see things in a different light,
and I see you
watching me
with a smile of acceptance on your face.

Eating cake, and finding forgiveness

1 John 1:9
But if we confess our sins to God, he can always be trusted
to forgive us and take our sins away.
(Contemporary English Version)

Every family has its stories and this is one of ours. Years ago, I had been baking the usual chocolate cake, which is always guaranteed to get the kids running into the kitchen wanting to lick the spoon. Jessie, I think, was about five or six at the time and hovered as close to the bowl as she could, watching as I emptied the mixture into the tin.

Once finished, the iced cake was placed on top of the piano out of temptation's way, or so I thought. I was simply trying to stop the dog from taking a bite.

Later that day, I found the cake with most of the icing gone, and very obvious fingermarks all over it. Confronting Jessie and Sam did no good as their denial was remarkably convincing in spite of the evidence in front of them. I had to let the matter rest.

Fast-forward twelve years and we are moving the piano into the newly extended kitchen. Along with lots of other rubbish that had collected behind it, I found a small note in felt-tip pen, in a childish hand, saying,

> *'deer mummy I am soooo soooo sorry. It was me that ate the icing. Pleeease forgive me. I love you soooo much. Jessie xxxxx'*

It seemed so funny finding the note like that, and I love the fact that she did own up, in her own way. Strangely, I realised yesterday that Jessie must have been waiting for me to find the note and then to tell her off.
I hope she assumed I had forgiven her, and carried on believing that I was a wonderful mum!

And that's what God does. He forgives us, and it's as if it's all forgotten, dropping away into the sea, never to be remembered again. We are the ones who tend to hold on, the ones who beat ourselves up over and over again, not able to forgive ourselves.

Jessie and I laugh about that story. I love her desire to tell the truth. She knows she is forgiven, and it's so important that we know we are.

Lord,
I think I use it as an excuse,
saying I'm not good enough,
thinking of my past
and the things I've done
that disqualify me from fully
serving you.
You say you have forgotten,
and I wish I could,
so completely
and utterly.

Lord give me grace,
to forgive myself,
and embrace the freedom
and joy of living in the present,
with you.

Angels in my kitchen

Hebrews 1:14
Are not the angels all ministering spirits (servants) sent out in the service [of God for the assistance] of those who are to inherit salvation?
(*Amplified Bible*)

I have an angel in my kitchen. Well, not a real one. She's more of the homemade variety and is made of cloth, a red and blue patterned dress over thick red felt, an embroidered apron and gold-metal wings. She has long woolly hair and hangs from the light fitting at the end of our large table. She makes me smile if I bump into her as I walk by. I can't remember where she comes from, but it doesn't really matter, she is just there.

My friend, Katy, says she has angels in her kitchen. The real ones this time. She spends a lot of time in her kitchen, praying and singing, and says that sometimes she can sense their presence. Now I can't prove that either way, and neither can she, but sometimes when I visit, the presence of God in her kitchen is palpable. I like to think she is right – the angels are there.

I do believe in angels, I think I've heard them singing. There have been times at church when the volume of sound from our singing seems too great for the number present. There is a quality to the sound that seems 'other-worldly', coming perhaps from a different dimension, another realm.

There are plenty of verses in the Bible about angels. They seem to be very active, and can speak, sing, protect, fight, search, and deliver messages anywhere and everywhere. So why shouldn't they be in a kitchen?

It's easy to dismiss these sorts of ideas that perhaps don't always fit our theology and we can be quick to dismiss unusual spiritual experiences. It's good to be cautious. We are told to 'test' and 'discern' the truth, but let's not dismiss things we don't understand just because they are not our experience. Yet.

We might even have an angel visit our own kitchen, so don't let's miss it.

Lord, keep me grounded
in the reality of life around me,
but don't let me lose hold of
the mystery
that is you.
Help me to allow space for the
unbelievable,
to welcome the unexpected,
and to allow you to be
fully God in my life.

A thin place

Psalm 9:1-2

I will praise you, Lord, with all my heart; I will tell of all the wonderful things you have done. I will sing with joy because of you.

(Good News Translation)

One summer, a few years ago now, we were in the grounds of the church of St Mary, on Holy Island, Northumberland. A blue day where sky floats on sea, and all seems well with the world. We walked from the mainland over soft brown mud-flats following the gentle line of the wind-seasoned way-markers that have stood for many years.

A straggled line of slow-moving pilgrims, like an uneven necklace of multi-coloured beads, we made our way, stepping through salt-sea puddles, singing songs and praying, looking in the water in the hope of hidden shells.

J. Hawke.

On reaching the island we sat in the sun, our pilgrim banner standing sentry in the sand beside us. We ate our lunch in quiet company. We had come for A Day of Quiet, led by my father, Eddie Askew, on behalf of The Leprosy Mission. Perhaps you were there?

I don't remember all that happened that day, but I do remember the atmosphere. It was a 'place apart'. The air was different. There was a palpable peace, a restfulness in the presence of many, a gentle joy. "This is a thin place," Dad said. A place where prayer has broken through the atmosphere, year after year, bringing a mysterious and permanent change.

Since that day much has changed in my life and probably in yours. But I remember that day, for the peace I felt, and the mystery of the island. I experienced God that day with many others, sitting on the grass, listening, singing, praying.

I have learnt to cling to those transcendent times when the space between heaven and earth embodies that 'thin place' when all that separates us is a gossamer-thin film, and heaven is a tangible reality. We can feel and touch a piece of heaven.

This is what sustains us, through the darkness, when heaven and all its comfort seems absent, we remember. We remember that on that day, in that particular place, we touched heaven.

Like Jacob of old, who was allowed to see angels and archangels ascending and descending. Like David who danced for sheer love of you. Oh that I could experience that now! But until then, I remember, and pray, and wait for the next 'thin place'.

> Lord,
> when I remember those times,
> my heart is full.
> I am so grateful for the 'thin
> places' in my life,
> when I have felt your breath on
> my face,
> and known that you are near.
> You draw me on, day by day
> asking me to search for you with
> all my heart,
> and to live my life in the light of
> your love.
> For there is nothing better,
> nothing more precious,
> than being with you.

Mortimer and the sheep

Nehemiah 8:10
The joy that the Lord gives you will make you strong.
(*Good News Translation*)

We were enjoying a walk with friends, by the side of a peaceful canal in Surrey, with deep water and the occasional duck to one side, and brambles, nettles and an old ruin to the other. Then we reached some open fields. The sole occupant of the nearest field was a rather bedraggled white sheep. We stopped; no I'll rephrase that, we were dragged to a stop by our dog, Mortimer. He is a rather too large and too shaggy white Labradoodle who should have known better than to grow quite so big. He is, in fact, about the size of a sheep, and I have a horrible suspicion that he is still growing.

So, we stood and watched them as they stood and watched each other, the dog and the sheep. I am certain I could hear their thought processes as they stood and stared.

> Mortimer: "Hey! Another Labradoodle, let's play."
> The sheep: "What's that sheep doing on the wrong side
>   of the fence?"

It was one of those split-second moments when life pauses and a memory is created. I'm sure neither the dog nor the sheep still think of it, but I still tell the story, and it continues to make me smile. We could so easily have missed it.

Let's not be too busy to notice the small things in life in our rush to get through the day.

Lord,
remind me to stop
and stand still occasionally,
even when time is short
and I'm feeling rushed.
Teach me to slow my breath,
to pause and watch,
and notice
the richness and joy
of life around me.

Honesty, the best policy?

Ephesians 4:15–16
Love should always make us tell the truth. Then we will grow in every way and be more like Christ, the head of the body.
(Contemporary English Version)

I know a very special little girl. She is five years old and her name is Grace and she has a wonderful way about her that seems older than her years. My grandmother would have said, "She's been here before!"

I was cooking lunch for her and her brother, heating the hot oil in the pan ready to roast some potatoes. I was aware that she was watching me with interest. Now, I can cook, but timing is not always my strong point, so let's fast-forward a bit. My attention had drifted onto something else when

the smoke alarm started to sound, very loudly. At the same time I noticed smoke pouring from the oven. The next five minutes were a blur, but I do remember a voice calmly asking, "Are we burning, Jenny?"

We got rid of the smoke, cooled the fat down and slid the aforementioned potatoes into the oven safely. All the time, Grace was calmly watching me at a safe distance. With her hands on her hips (remember she is only two-and-a-half feet tall), and, shaking her head, she said, with all the innocence of a child, "You're really not very good at this cooking thing, are you, Jenny?"

It was more of an observation than a criticism. A statement of fact, with no malice in it at all. I had to admit that on this occasion my timing really wasn't that brilliant. What was the point of trying to defend myself against such an honest and kindly meant statement?

We had a good lunch, the potatoes tasted great, and the smoke was not mentioned again. I guess it served to remind me that children often speak the truth when we might not. And it was done with such a lovely smile, I didn't mind at all. I think we could all do with hearing a bit more truth, especially when spoken in love.

The truth spoken in love,
Lord,
that's not an easy thing to do.
At times I know that you
highlight
something in my life,
asking me to look again
and notice the need
for change.
My opinions, my actions,
you see it all.
But you ask no more than I
can give,
and with a gentleness that I
don't always deserve
you wait for me to ask for
your help.

Life is good, Lord,
to be savoured and enjoyed,
just like the roast potatoes.
Help me to see you through
the smoke
and debris of my mistakes
and learn from you.

The enthusiasm of the young

John 5:19

So Jesus answered them,"I tell you the truth: the Son can do nothing on his own;
he does only what he sees his Father doing. What the Father does, the Son also
does." (*Good News Translation*)

I teach Pilates. In case you don't know, it's a system of exercise that is very
helpful and safe for people with back and neck problems and I've been
teaching for a number of years. One member of my Monday evening class
has a little girl. I think she's about three years old.

On this particular night, the young mother was just getting ready to leave
when she noticed her daughter standing patiently by the front door. Nothing
unusual about that, except that she had her backpack on over her pyjamas.
When asked what she was doing, she said, 'I'm ready to come to Pilates with
you Mummy.'

Three years old and bursting with enthusiasm. I don't think for one moment
that she thought she might be too young, or not allowed to go because it
was past her bedtime… She saw Mummy going to Pilates week after week
and she wanted to do what Mummy was doing.

At class we all laughed and wished that she could have come along. It would
have added an extra dimension, but what struck me was that she had
noticed something Mummy was doing
and wanted to copy her.

That's exactly what Jesus did – he
copied his Father – and as Christians,
that's the way we are supposed to
live too. The Bible talks about us
living intentionally, not carelessly,
a sobering thought sometimes, but
also a thought with much potential for
joy. It's a matter of loving someone so
much that we can't help but want to
be with them and live like them, just
like the little girl and her mum.

Lord, my problem is
life gets in the way.
I forget,
and don't notice where you are
and what you might be doing,
in my place of work,
at home,
with my friends.
Help me to see with your eyes
and listen to what you are saying
to me today.
Then, full of faith and enthusiasm
and always ready for joy,
let me follow close behind you.

Things aren't always what they seem

1 John 4:18

'There is no fear in love [dread does not exist], but full-grown (complete, perfect) love turns fear out of doors and expels every trace of terror!

(*Amplified Bible*)

I grew up in India. For the first ten years of my life we lived in a place called Purulia, just west of Calcutta, or Kolkata as it is now known. My older sister and I were free to play outside our large garden, roaming paddy fields, and looking for frogs in the tiny pond over the road.

When Steph was sent to boarding school, I spent more time on my own and loved wandering the dusty road outside our mission house. I don't remember being afraid, or at least not until the time of day when dusk was approaching. I think we used to call it '*Go-dhouli* time'. If anyone speaks Bengali, please correct me if I'm wrong, but it was the time of day when the cows came home and I think the expression is translated as 'the dust of the cows in the last rays of the sun'.

The cows would shamble along our road from the fields where they had spent the day, kicking up clouds of dust, picking up some speed, and making quite a noise, or at least it seemed that way to a six-year-old child. The only problem was that I thought they were following me. Convinced they were speeding up with the sole purpose of catching me, I would run for home with my heart pounding in my chest. I wouldn't feel safe until I had opened our large wooden gate and slammed the large metal latch down behind me. I could then watch them pass by in safety.

Looking back I wonder why I never told Mum about my fears. It never occurred to me that the cows were simply going home. It's so easy to feel fearful when we don't need to, when we don't know all the facts and misinterpret the situation. All I needed was to share my fears and someone would have put me right.

The Bible tells us not to be afraid over a hundred times. God places a lot of emphasis on this subject. He knows we are human and open to doubts and fears just as much as we are open to his love and compassion. I guess growing up, physically and spiritually, means getting a sense of proportion and choosing to turn fear out of doors.

> Lord, sometimes my fears get the better of me,
> looming larger than life itself,
> and blocking my view of the truth.
> You tell me, "Do not fear",
> and I would agree
> if only I could do it.
> Lord, help my unbelief,
> wrap me in your love,
> take my hand
> and teach me.

A coat with deep pockets

Philippians 3:13-14

… the one thing I do, however, is to forget what is behind me and do my best to reach what is ahead. So I run straight toward the goal in order to win the prize, which is God's call through Christ Jesus to the life above.

(*Good News Translation*)

I'm not sure if I am a natural optimist or a pessimist. My husband would say it depends on what time of day you speak to me. I don't find mornings easy, especially in the winter when the sun seems to linger so often behind a blanket of grey. A sense of pessimism can creep up on you and, before you realise it, everything looks the same colour. I had a year like that recently.

As a family we had had several painful losses in a short space of time, and things in my work were not going as well as hoped. God seemed very distant and I was aware of a heaviness that was colouring everything I did. I prayed, I exercised, I even ate chocolate to boost my spirits, but little changed. Then, one day, I suddenly saw in my mind a picture of myself wearing a rather strange, long and flapping coat. It seemed to have pockets everywhere, many of which were full, others, empty, but the overall effect was that it was weighing me down very heavily. I seemed to hear the words, 'disappointment is a coat with deep pockets'. A strange picture but it explained so much. I had been holding on to each disappointment, and waiting for more so I could fill the empty pockets too.

Stuff happens. Life can be so hard, but Paul teaches us to move on, to process what happens to us in a healthy way, and then leave it behind.

This was all I had to do. To let go. And it felt so good when I did.

Lord, I think it would be good
if you called me in for a
regular check.
A spiritual MOT.
Just like my car.
To see how I am,
check for damage,
look for signs of scarring
or wear and tear.

I need renewal, Lord,
your love washing over me,
taking away the dust
of yesterday,
and making me ready
for the challenge of tomorrow.

A foot-sized fire-engine

Matthew 18:3

Truly I say to you, unless you repent (change, turn about) and become
like little children [trusting, lowly, loving, forgiving], you can never
enter the kingdom of heaven [at all].

(*Amplified Bible*)

I've just got back home after helping to walk three lovely children to school.
Helping to get them ready beforehand is always fun. My children are grown
up now and it's so easy to forget what it's like inside the mind of a child.

I was playing with the youngest girl, Grace, who loves Peppa Pig and Fireman
Sam so we were putting Peppa Pig into Fireman Sam's fire engine. Grace
suddenly shouts, "Look, I can get my foot inside the fire engine!" Not the
entire foot, but most of it. She was so pleased.

The question remains, and I did ask her, why would you want to get your
foot inside the fire engine, but that's a question from an adult perspective,
and Grace had no answer for me. It was very evident that she was having
fun, and that's the point I was missing.

Jesus loved being around children
and I can imagine them rushing
to him, climbing all over him and
generally getting in the way. At
least, that's what the disciples
seemed to think. Children have a
way of seeing things differently;
they have different agendas, mainly
linked to lots of laughter and having
fun. As a grown-up, it's too easy
for me to miss this. Grace saw an
opportunity to have some fun,
and use her wonderful imagination
and so that's what she did.

Let's see if we can look at this day
through the eyes of a child. We
might just discover something new.

Lord, imagination is a
wonderful thing,
unless it's like mine,
often running out of control,
careering down tracks
I wish it wouldn't take,
seeing disaster
around every corner.

Lord, will you change my
perspective?
I need a different view on life,
some lateral thinking,
and time for fun.
Please lighten my spirit,
give me the freedom to live
with joy and laughter today.

Where the seagulls go

John 14:2

In my Father's house are many rooms; if it were not so, I would have told you. I am going there to prepare a place for you. (*New International Version*)

If I look up into the sky, on any day whenever dusk is approaching, I see an amazing sight. Line upon line of seagulls high in the sky all heading in the same direction. Hundreds of them. I've tried working out which direction they always take and I think it is towards the east, but since I don't have a very good sense of direction, as my husband will testify, I could easily be proved wrong.

I watch each flock of birds in awe, not only at their huge numbers, but also at the neat staggered 'V' formations they fly in. It is a sight worth seeing.

One day, a couple of years ago, I sat in Esher and watched for more than twenty minutes. I began counting the birds but soon gave up when I reached two hundred. And I always ask myself the same question, 'Where do they go to?' I know they are going home, to nests of some sort, in which to safely rest till morning returns, but I'm curious as to where these are in my area.

The homing instinct is such a strong one and home is a precious place. I am blessed by mine. Jesus said that whilst he was on earth, he didn't have a home, but he talked of going away to prepare a place for us. The important thing is that, as Christians, we are all headed in the same direction, following him home, in whichever way he is leading us, to his father's house.

Lord, the homing instinct is a strong one,
drawing us back to our place of safety.
Keep me close, Lord,
following right behind you,
wherever you lead.
Through the darkness and the light,
lead me always towards home.
For you and you only
are my beginning
and my end.

One by one

Matthew 25:35-36
For I was hungry and you gave me something to eat, I was thirsty and you gave me something to drink, I was a stranger and you invited me in, I needed clothes and you clothed me, I was sick and you looked after me, I was in prison and you came to visit me. (*New International Version*)

Sometimes, when I watch the news, I feel almost paralysed by the enormity of need I see on the screen. Sometimes I even change channels. Situations can seem so desperate and I am at a loss as to what to do but pray. I am not meaning to diminish the power of prayer, but there is so much else I feel I should be doing. So much so, that I often end up doing very little at all.

Recently, I was preparing a talk that I was to give about The Leprosy Mission, and that was when I realised…

It only takes one.
One person to start something.
One person to do some kindness.
Right here, where I am, I can do one thing to make a difference to someone else.

Wellesley Bailey, the founder of the Mission, was only one man. He noticed a need, and began something small that has grown to what we now know as The Leprosy Mission.

I have a lovely friend, Denise. She is a tennis coach who felt she wanted to use her tennis skills in Africa to teach underprivileged children. She simply turned up with some tennis racquets and some balls and now, four years later, she has raised over £100,000 for the ongoing support and education of 32 children in an orphanage in Uganda. It's called 'Daniel's Promise'. What she has done is inspiring. It only takes one. One person to start something.

And we can help people one by one as well. Let God highlight who and when and where, and who knows how he will use us.

Let's change things. One by one.

Lord, I don't want to make excuses anymore.
Time is short,
and though I am faced
with such great need,
please use the little I have.
Like the loaves and the fishes,
and my mustard seed of faith,
I know you can make small things grow
into mighty oaks of opportunity.

Colossians 3:12
You are the people of God; he loved you and chose you for his own.
(*Good News Translation*)

J. Hawke.

My son can get a bit irritated when I attribute various human emotions to our dog. There's little scientific proof, he says. That may be so, but what I see on a daily basis makes me think otherwise.

Our very hairy, white Labradoodle is very affectionate. He gets excited when I return after a five-minute absence, giving me the privilege of his 'full-body wag', which means he is more than usually happy. And now it appears he is in love.

Last year, we met a beautiful, shaggy, black dog named Rosie. From the moment they met, there seemed to be something special going on. They ran around in ever-decreasing circles and ended up lying on the grass together licking each other's faces. If we see Rosie and her lovely owners about 300 yards away in our local park, we have only to say, "Where's Rosie?" and Mortimer's ears prick up before he launches himself in the direction of the black shape on the horizon. When she sees him, she does the same. I am reminded of that familiar slow-motion scene in a film where a couple run towards each other on a beach! Rosie's owners assure us that she isn't like this with any other dog.

Now I'm pretty sure that I can't really equate what humans feel when 'in love' to what Rosie and Morty are feeling, but it does remind me of what a wonderful thing it is to love and be loved. And, whatever our human experience is, the love of God is worth running towards, and holding onto.

Lord, you made us as we are,
needing to love and be loved.
Complete only in you,
you gave us the ultimate gift,
the life of your son,
who, holding nothing back,
loved beyond reason.
And now we are loved,
unconditionally,
joyously,
so generously.
Thank you.
Thank you.
Thank you.

Lost in translation

Isaiah 50:4
The Sovereign Lord has taught me what to say, so that I can strengthen the weary.
Every morning he makes me eager to hear what he is going to teach me.
(*Good News Translation*)

I was asked to teach a course in Lithuania last year. A great opportunity to experience a different culture and a chance for a few days away with my husband, Peter. My boss assured me that although I would have a translator, I wouldn't really need him as the students would all speak some English. I could relax.

Unfortunately this wasn't the case. Only one person out of 25 spoke any English, so everything I said had to be translated. One or two sentences, then a pause while it was translated. Lithuanian seems to have a lot more words than we do, or that is what it felt like. I had to think in a totally different way before I spoke. It was hard work.

My father travelled a lot and sometimes spent hours in international meetings. He would be given earphones so everything could be translated into English for him. He admitted to me that once, when he was bored, he surreptitiously put in his own earphones, so he could listen to Brahms' violin concerto and still look like he was listening to the group.

The language we use as Christians is important and it can either put up barriers or bring understanding. We have a wonderful message of hope. Let's not lose any part of it in translation, but instead, like Jesus, let's try to speak with a clear and joyful relevance to life today. Then our message will capture people's attention, without them wanting to tune in to Brahms as an alternative.

Lord, you spoke honestly, using pictures and everyday examples.
You chose the familiar and simple
to explain the immensity of your love.
Give me the grace to do the same,
waiting to hear from you before I rush in
with my own opinions, over-complicating the simple truth
that your gift is for everyone and your message is timeless.

A cat called Tadpole

Philippians 4:7
And the peace of God, which transcends all understanding, will guard your hearts and your minds in Christ Jesus. (*New International Version*)

We have a ginger cat called Tadpole. Yes, it's a very strange name. He was the runt of the litter and when he was born we thought his tail looked like a tadpole and so the name stuck. He hasn't been the luckiest of cats. When he was a year or two old he was run over by a lorry, and left on the ground with tyre marks over his body. And yet he survived, despite fractures in his pelvis, left front leg and some bladder damage. He seemed to purr his way through the long recovery and yes, we did pray for him. He also lost his tail. I wanted to re-christen him 'Frog' but Peter wasn't keen. I didn't think there was much difference in how embarrassed we would feel shouting out 'Frog' rather than 'Tadpole' when we were calling him in from the garden.

Unfortunately, he wasn't insured – the cat that is, not the husband – but that's another story as to how our marriage survived the enormous bills we were given by the vet!

Anyway, Tadpole is now 15 and an Olympic sleeper. He is a bit on the rotund side, eating well and storing all the energy he needs to sleep through the night, get up to have breakfast and then sleep through the day, until it's tea time and the cycle begins again. You have to admire his focus. He is a happy cat, except when I throw him out for an hour in the cold. I guess he is happy, sleeping and eating and enjoying the peace of the later years of his life just as much as he enjoyed the adventures of his youth. He is and always has been, a model of contentment.

Now I know there is a world of difference between our lives and the things we may go through, and the life of a cat, but I am reminded of the deep contentment that comes from having the peace of God in our lives. And he promises us an 'otherworldly' peace which, despite our outward circumstances, stays deep within, helping us through.

Lord, thank you
for the promise of your peace,
as companion in this life,
staying with me
regardless of circumstance,
in wind and storm,
in calm and plenty,
your peace enfolds
and holds me still.

Folding socks

Matthew 28:20
And surely I am with you always, to the very end of the age.
(*New International Version*)

It's funny the things we do without thinking, just out of habit. Things we have done for years, and now we forget why. A few years ago, Dad told us a funny story. He was travelling for The Leprosy Mission and had come to the end of the day. Before getting into bed, he took off his socks and suddenly became aware that he was folding them very carefully before putting them down on his chair.

Now that in itself might not strike you as weird, but it was something he always did, and had done so for over 40 years. The reason behind it made us all smile.

When Dad was a youngster during the war, being a tidy person, he noticed that on the nights when he took time to fold his socks, there wasn't an air-raid. If he forgot, it seemed there was always a raid. In his innocence, he decided that the fate of his neighbourhood lay in his hands and so he continued to deliberately fold his socks night after night. Over the years it became a habit. I wonder about the enormous power of Dad's socks? Did they save lives? Change the course of the war? Of course not, but the funny thing is that all through his life he continued to fold them.

As a young boy, Dad put his trust in folding his socks, and we can tend to do the same, like crossing our fingers, or touching wood. The great thing is that we have a God more powerful than anything else. Jesus doesn't say that we won't experience trouble, but that he will always be with us. He wants us to depend on him. That sounds a lot safer to me than folding socks.

Lord, it must make you smile
to see the things I do
to control my life.
Holding on
when I should let go.
Forgetting your promises,
always with me,
before and behind.

Alpha and Omega,
forgive me,
and lead me on
today and every day.

Romans 15:4
And the Scriptures give us hope and encouragement as we wait patiently
for God's promises to be fulfilled.
(*New Living Translation*)

I went through a hard time a few years back. I had been experiencing chronic pain from a back problem for over three years and had become clinically depressed as a result. Coming out of it, but still with the pain, I found it hard to hold on to a sense of hope. I was lucky or, I should say, blessed in having good friends and a loving family to support me. One of them said one day, "Don't forget God's promises to you; stand on the promises."

I think she was quite brave in saying that to me, but then she is one of my best friends, and has always told me the truth as she sees it. The quote comes from a beautiful old hymn* by Russell Kelso Carter, which I remember from my childhood.

> 'Standing, standing, standing on the promises of God my Saviour, Standing, standing, I'm standing on the promises of God.'

Some may think it sacrilegious, but I decided to take this literally, so I wrote two Bible verses on small pieces of paper and put one in each shoe. Every day from then on, I was literally standing on the promises of God. It served to remind me of God's words to me in spite of apparent circumstances.

As time went on, I changed the pieces of paper for other verses, and found I was coming out of the darkness. My faith had survived. I have a feeling that God would like us to take Him a little more literally. At least some of the time.

*There is a YouTube clip of a man called Alan Jackson singing 'Standing on the Promises of God,' if you want to listen. It's beautiful.

Lord, thank you
that in the hardest times
you were there,
through the tears and despair,
you brought me through
to a better place.
For surely I have a delightful
inheritance
and the lines have fallen for me
in pleasant places.
Your word
is life to me.
There is no one but you.

Taking the long way home

'Are you tired? Worn out? Burned out on religion? Come to me. Get away with me and you'll recover your life. I'll show you how to take a real rest. Walk with me and work with me – watch how I do it. Learn the unforced rhythms of grace. I won't lay anything heavy or ill-fitting on you. Keep company with me and you'll learn to live freely and lightly.'

(*The Message*)

I tend to take the shortest way wherever I am going. I am so geared up to saving time that I do it automatically even though I'm not sure what I am saving time for. As a child in India, we lived in a lovely whitewashed bungalow which had a driveway all around it, with the garage in one corner. When Dad drove in, he would drive round to the right of the house, with us all expecting him to then turn left into the garage, but sometimes, at the last minute, he would swing the steering wheel to the right, and begin the circuit around the house once more. We would all scream with delight, and beg him to do it again, and again.

Taking the long way home. That's all he was doing. Giving us the anticipation of some fun even when he and Mum were probably tired. Now when Peter and I are driving back from a walk in the country, we will decide to come the long way home, the more scenic route that may take a little longer but is always worth the extra time.

I once read a book called *Slowing Down to the Speed of Life* by Richard Carlson and Joseph Bailey. I picked it up solely for the title. The idea that I could slow down, and that life was really meant to be slower than we make it, appealed to my weary self. This good book taught me again that we don't need to rush, that we often set unnecessary deadlines for ourselves, when what we really need is to take the long way home.

Give yourself space today to take the scenic route, go slowly and enjoy the experience.

Thank you God for laughter, for those glorious moments that break into my day, bringing welcome relief to my busy life. Keep company with me Lord, teach me to walk with the rhythm of your grace. Teach me to see what you see. Let me take the scenic route with you.

John 6:9

"There's a little boy here who has
five barley loaves and two fish.
But that's a drop in the bucket
for a crowd like this."

(*The Message*)

I was looking at this passage the other day with some friends of mine. It's funny how you can be so familiar with the story and yet still something new will hit you.

You can imagine it, can't you? The little boy running up to Jesus with his hands full of the family lunch. "I've got some, here, you can have mine."

He had overheard the discussion between Jesus and his disciples. He felt he had the answer and so he ran forwards. I wonder, did he ask his mum, or was she watching, with her heart sinking, as she saw the only food they had brought, disappear into the crowd.

Philip looked at the numbers, saw the immediate and incredible need, and the little resources they had. "Two hundred pennies worth of bread is not enough." Apparently a sum equal to two months' wages. The boy heard Jesus and offered what he had.

How do we explain the mystery of what happened next, except by saying it was miraculous? Jesus took what was offered, blessed it, and thousands were fed.

Neil, the minister of our church, said last week that many of us feel we have nothing to offer God, and therefore feel disqualified from serving him. "But," he added, "if you are a Christian, and you have a pulse, then you're qualified." What a relief. I can do all things through Christ who strengthens me. I just need to be willing, offer him my loaves and fish, and leave the rest to him.

Lord, I'm ready.
No more excuses.
Let's go,
with the little I have
and the power you give,
we'll make a good team.

Hugging Dad

Psalm 30:11
You have changed my sadness into a joyful dance; you have taken away my sorrow
and surrounded me with joy. (*Good News Translation*)

Grief is a strange thing. It seems to come in cycles. John Mumford, our
former church minister, described it as 'orbiting planets, hitting you
when you least expect it'. Over three years after losing my parents, some
memories are as raw as they ever were, but occasionally, very occasionally,
something wonderful happens. I dream of Mum and Dad. My dreams are
very vivid, and twice now I have dreamt that they were back.

The last time, I was standing with friends when I saw Dad ahead of me.
I ran towards him and threw my arms around him. He hugged me and I said
to him, "Are you staying?" He simply smiled and kept hugging me. He felt
utterly real and looked so well. When I woke, I could still see and feel him,
and the hug kept me smiling for a very long time. It was so real.

Now I am not an expert on dreams, but I am so grateful to God that
I do dream, and that I can experience something so real and so helpful.
God is good, and his timing
continues to amaze me.
We all need his encouragement.

Terry Waite was imprisoned
for nearly five years, chained
in a dark cell, and said that
his dreams during that time
'were rich and comforting'.
God knows our needs so
well and often answers our
prayers in unexpected and
amazing ways, through dreams,
or a phone call, a card, an e-mail.
We too can be part of God's
answer to someone's prayer by
responding in the smallest of ways.

Lord, it's been so hard,
these few years
without my parents.
We thought we were prepared,
but life has been smaller,
our family so much diminished
by the enormity of loss.
I am grateful
for memories,
and photographs
and all that reminds us of them.
And thank you,
thank you for my dream.
It was so real.
In my heart I danced
and I knew I was loved.
Thank you.

Three shillings for a punch on the nose

Galatians 6:9

So let's not get tired of doing what is good. At just the right time we will reap a harvest of blessing if we don't give up.

(*New Living Translation*)

The law is a strange and complicated thing. Since my son, Sam, has been studying it, we have become more aware of the history behind our present-day British Law. Apparently in the 600s if you punched someone on the nose, you were fined three shillings. Quite a lot of money in those days. Ten shillings for taking someone's eye out. I'll stop there before it gets too gruesome. The point is, the law was the law and you paid for what you did with what was considered to be an appropriate punishment.

I was very talkative as a child and was often in trouble in class for talking too much. I had to stand outside the headmaster's office numerous times waiting to see him. He was a jovial man and would simply stick his head out

of his door, smile at me and say "Oh it's you again, Jenny." I don't remember much else except being told not to do it again. He realised the anxiety of the wait was punishment enough.

Like any loving parent, God prefers to reward his children rather than punish them. In Galatians, it says we will reap what we sow, and whilst I am aware of the mercy and grace of God, I know that how I act is my responsibility. It's easy to lose heart when our actions seem to be having no impact on the world around us, but God promises that if we do not tire of doing good, then we will reap a harvest of blessings, at just the right time.

And maybe there's my problem. I want results now, and when the 'right time' seems long in coming, I get impatient. I need to remember that God's timing is always better than mine.

Lord, resilience is a great word.
Strong,
enduring,
never giving up.
In fact, a lot like love.
Would you give me the resilience I need
to keep on sowing,
without losing heart,
and to keep on believing
that your perfect timing will come.

Changing the baby

2 Corinthians 4:16-18

Therefore we do not lose heart... For our light and momentary troubles are achieving for us an eternal glory that far outweighs them all. So we fix our eyes not on what is seen, but on what is unseen. For what is seen is temporary, but what is unseen is eternal. (*New International Version*)

I was in the supermarket today, just popping in to use their loos. I passed the doors on the right showing the way to the Gents, then the loo for the disabled and lastly the door to the baby-changing room. I giggled, picturing it literally. A place where you could go and exchange your squalling, red-faced and not very pretty baby for a new one, a different model! A quiet, well-behaved one. A baby that would sleep when you wanted it to, the second its downy head touched the pillow. A baby that would always smile when it woke and who would eat whatever you gave it.

And then I thought, what would happen to all the old unwanted models? Could they be recycled? Or even retrained and you might come back for them later. And what if the changing rooms worked for husbands too? On those days when all you seem to do is argue over the smallest things, and the honeymoon is well and truly over, what would it be like to simply go and ask for another? Trade him in and walk away with a different model. Life is getting a bit like that anyway. The TV or the hoover breaks down, and no one thinks it's worth mending them. Buy another. A better version.

However hard life gets, let's take a step back. It's important to fully appreciate what we already have. The baby that won't stop crying will be taking her A-levels soon enough, and I'll be wishing she was small again, however noisy. The husband who occasionally irritates me is God's gift to me for life and He loves me. The tough times will pass.

Lord, where did those years go? It feels like yesterday, giving kisses for bruised knees, feeling chubby arms around my neck, and the sweet smell of childhood days. It's easy to wish it away, and now I wish I could do it all again. Thank you Lord, that you have made my life the richer with opportunities to love and be loved. Help me to accept the passage of time, and to live fully, today.

Guinea pigs on the loose

Matthew 19:13-14

Some people brought their children to Jesus, so that he could place his hands on them and pray for them. His disciples told the people to stop bothering him. But Jesus said, "Let the children come to me, and don't try to stop them! People who are like these children belong to God's kingdom."

(Contemporary English Version)

Growing up in India in a large house with a very large garden meant we were able to have numerous pets. Apparently Dad had always wanted to build a zoo, but Mum made sure we stuck to smaller animals, such as dogs, cats and guinea pigs.

Anyway, back to the guinea pigs. We had about 15 of them, kept in a large pen in the garden. One day, and I can't remember why, they got out. Someone must have left the cover off. What I do remember is the amazing sight of 15 excited guinea pigs tearing around the garden, making the most of their freedom, whilst five or six adults and two children ran after them.

For me it was the highlight of the day. It took an hour or so to get them all under control, and probably a further half hour for Mum and Dad to calm down and get back to work. It looked like fun to me, aged five, and it certainly seemed like fun to the escapees. It all depends on your perspective.

It's like putting a new pair of glasses on; it gives you a better focus on what you see. Children are good at that, seeing the joy rather than the nuisance in a situation. I can see why Jesus loved the company of children, as a welcome relief from the misunderstanding he was sometimes surrounded with. He loved their lightness of spirit that we as adults can so easily lose. I guess we need a balance, recognising the reality of the situation in front of us, but also having a lighter heart within. Whether it's guinea pigs or a day at the office, let's try seeing with a different perspective, through the eyes of a child.

Lord, I'd love to keep my sense of fun in all things,
seeing the lighter side of life,
but I get tired,
disappointed with the way things have worked out.
Help me to let go
of the burden of worry
that obscures my view of life,
replacing it with
your sense of fun and joy.

The good old days

Hebrews 13:8-9
Jesus Christ is the same yesterday, today, and forever. So do not be
attracted by strange, new ideas...
(*New Living Translation*)

It's easy to look back and think everything was easier in 'the old days'.
Life was better and people were happier. The world was just a nicer place
to be. Whilst this might be true for a few things, many things have changed
for the better.

My sister and I were born into the 'Dr Spock' days of child rearing. Things
were done in a routine and ordered fashion, and if the baby cried, so long as
it wasn't hungry, cold or wet, he or she would be left alone.

And there lay the problem. Stephanie had been crying for a little while, and
Mum told the *ayah*, our Indian nursemaid, to ignore her. She had, as they
say, been fed and watered. The crying persisted and got louder and louder
but Mum's faith in Dr Spock was firmly rooted. She was resolute in spite of
the *ayah* saying, "But Memsahib, the baby?"

Since the crying did not stop, Mum reluctantly went out to see what was
wrong. Her horror at seeing the pram overturned and her baby in the
shallow gutter below the verandah, was only matched by the look of disdain
on the *ayah*'s face. She took the baby out of Mum's arms and walked away
back into the house. I think there was a relaxing of the 'bible according to
Dr Spock' that day.

Fashions come and go, and we do our best at the time with what we know.
It's the same with our faith, I think. Years ago my faith had far fewer
questions and many more answers than it does now, but that in itself
doesn't worry me. I feel my experience over the years has deepened my love
for God despite the increasing number of questions. My faith has developed,
and hopefully matured.

Dr Spock may not be so relevant now, but my faith still is, every day and in
every circumstance. Things have changed, but God remains. His love for me
is unconditional and he is more steadfast, more faithful and more enduring
than any fashion, theory or question. And that is good enough for me.

Lord, fashions come and go,
theories rise and fall,
and faith is called into question
but I know you never change.
Your love, like a rock,
supports,
defends,
protects,
and lifts me up
closer to you.
Thank you.

An audience of one

John 7:38

Have faith in me, and you will have life-giving water flowing from deep inside you, just as the Scriptures say.

(*Contemporary English Version*)

I believe it was John Wimber, founder of the Vineyard Churches, who coined the phrase, I live my life 'before an audience of one'. This journey, yours, mine, is before an audience of one, the One. Between you and Him, between me and Him. It's not for me to compare myself to you or vice-versa, our love is for Him and it spills out onto each other and onto an unsuspecting world. The more we love Him, the more we find ourselves loving each other.

Edwina Gateley, author and retreat leader, writes, 'We who have received the love of Christ through the spirit cannot contain it. It must reach out to others, spilling out and touching the world in which we live.'

I love that idea of love spilling out, of being uncontainable within us. Being full of His love means we cannot contain it or ourselves. We have to spill. It seems a little easier that way; to live our lives by simply loving God. He will spill out of us. Less wearying perhaps than many of our complicated agendas and programmes.

Your steps in life are different from mine, but we are each making a unique mark on the ground beneath us. Let His enormous love fill you, and surround you as you move through your day.

> Lord, fill me to the brim,
> until I overflow.
> Bring life to this dry and dusty land.
> It sounds so simple,
> just to love you
> with all my heart,
> and everything else will follow.
> Life in all its abundance,
> flowing with your streams of living water.
> Lord, keep me thirsting
> so I'll always return to you.

Grandma's cake tins

Romans 12:13
When God's people are in need, be ready to help them.
Always be eager to practise hospitality.
(*New Living Translation*)

My mother-in-law was a wonderful cook, but more than that, she really knew how to feed us. She and my father-in-law lived in Swanage and over the years her home was a holiday break for us from our busy and tired lives.

Walking in the front doorway, Peter and I, our children, and the dog always rushed into the kitchen. Of course, we would hug and kiss Mary at the door, but the second joy was seeing the contents of her cake tins. They were numerous, and piled high on the old black range. We lifted lids, smelling and tasting before she could stop us. Rocky road, brownies, chocolate refrigerator cake, Victoria sponge, shortbread, coffee and walnut cake, rice crispy cakes, melting moments, and so it went, on and on.

Mary came from a generation of women who perhaps were taught not to show emotion easily, but she showed us her love through her cooking. Actions speak loud, don't they? Childhood memories are precious and she was so generous with her time and effort on our behalf.

Lord, it's easy to think
the little I do isn't worth much.
It won't change the world, will it,
making cupcakes?
But then I don't see the
bigger picture.
The welcoming smell of
baking bread,
and time given so freely,
speaks more than words
to my worn and weary soul.
Like the widow and her mite,
you see the heart,
and sometimes all I need to do
is trust you,
and keep on giving.

Now that she is gone, we talk often about those tins, and try to recreate the recipes though they never taste quite the same. I will always be grateful to Mary. She gave my children something precious. They have both inherited her love of baking, and my daughter, now at university, told me that she is carrying on the tradition. She bakes cupcakes and pizzas for her friends. Grandma would be proud.

Food helps friendships grow and hospitality can be catching. Let's pass it on.

Don't hold your breath, Brian!

Job 33:4

[It is] the Spirit of God that made me [which has stirred me up], and the breath of the Almighty that gives me life [which inspires me].

(Amplified Bible)

There's a lovely man called Brian in one of my Pilates classes. Now, Pilates isn't just about moving – it's about breathing too. Slow and steady breathing as we move is really important during the hour-long class. The trouble with Brian is that he forgets to breathe, so my normal instructions to the class are always peppered with shouts of 'Breathe, Brian, breathe!'

We joke that I can always tell when it's time for him to breathe as his ears tend to go very pink. He tells me it's because he is concentrating so hard on the movement, that he doesn't have time to breathe as well. I suspect he might also be holding his breath just waiting for the movement to be over.

It reminded me that when I was a lot younger, I seemed to be always waiting: for my problems to pass; holding my breath for the next big thing to happen; always wishing time away so my 'real life' could begin; seldom appreciating the present.

We can have that same attitude to our progress through our Christian life. We want to get to the good bits, the excitement, without the slow wait in between. We want to be holy now, displaying the fruits of the Spirit now. And we lose patience when we realise that we are not – not yet.

The work of God in us, of the Holy Spirit in us, is a long one, a work in progress. Day by day, month by month, we have to trust that He is being formed in us. And as we continue to look for Him in our daily lives, we are being made into His likeness.

Lord, it's too easy for me
to wish my life away,
holding my breath
for better days.
Longing for excitement
instead of hard times and
muscle strain.
I find it hard to just be,
yet so often
that is all you ask.
to be still,
and know that you are God.

Help me to enjoy you
now
in this moment
wherever I am
whatever I am doing.

Dancing in the rain

Psalm 100:1-3
Shout praises to the LORD, everyone on this earth. Be joyful and sing as you come
in to worship the LORD! You know the LORD is God! He created us, and we belong
to him; we are his people, the sheep in his pasture.
(*Contemporary English Version*)

Living in India could be hot and dry, and the monsoon season was longed for by everyone. As children in Purulia, we would watch the rainclouds gather and then we would smell it, that delicious fragrance of moisture in the air. Seeing the first drops hitting the dusty ground in front of the verandah was all the signal we needed. Steph and I would charge out into the garden shouting and screaming, arms in the air and faces turned towards the clouds above. I think Dad and Mum would join us too.

When the real downpour started I would head for the rapidly filling drains that ran around our bungalow, which were turning into what seemed to me to be raging torrents that I could paddle in. I felt very brave. Mum was of the opposite opinion, convinced I would catch worms (I never did) and trying to persuade me to come in. I don't think she tried very hard as I seldom did.

When my own children were little, we would do the same, enjoying a really good downpour of warm English summer rain, standing in the garden with mouths wide open trying to catch a raindrop. I've always encouraged them to jump in puddles too, providing they weren't too deep, figuring that a moment's joy is worth a few dirty clothes. Mud always washes out.

So the next time it's a clear night, pause and look up to the stars. When the robin sings, take a moment and be amazed. And when the rain pours down, jump in a puddle. It's moments like these that connect us to the beauty of the world around. We are so blessed.

Lord, if growing up means having
no fun
then you can keep it.
I want to stay young,
young enough to stop and stare,
to roll down hillsides,
and make snow angels
in fresh snow.
To jump in puddles,
enjoy toffee apples,
and hear the birds sing.

When the pressure of my life
threatens to rob me of my joy,
show me a puddle, Lord,
and remind me to jump.

Walking with lions

John 14:27

I give you peace, the kind of peace that only I can give. It isn't like the peace that this world can give. So don't be worried or afraid.

(Contemporary English Version)

Today my son has walked with lions. He is in Zimbabwe working as an intern for two months, and today he walked with lions! He rang to tell me, "They're just like big cats, Mum, and I stroked their heads."

Sam and I had an agreement before he left. 'If you are going to do anything dangerous, tell me about it afterwards.' That was my idea. To be honest, I wasn't at all happy that he was going there but he was determined and being over 21 meant I had little power to stop him. And there he was, having the experience of a lifetime and here I was shopping in Sainsbury's. Meanwhile, the rest of London was picking up the pieces after a week of intense rioting and other towns across the country were preparing themselves for the rioting to reach their high streets.

Life is strange, isn't it? I thought Sam would be in more danger out there in a country that has had a volatile political history, and rather more wild animals than we do, and yet here in England, the local shopkeepers were closing early to protect their shops from looting and violence.

For a moment there, I wondered who was in more danger, my son, or me? Either way I am just happy that the lions weren't hungry.

Lord,
wherever I go today,
walk with me.
Be close when lions and other dangers threaten,
whether real or imagined,
keep my mind settled in your peace.
For I know that I can never be separated
from your love
in Christ Jesus.

Jerry Hawke '04

A doll with no eyelashes

1 John 1:9
But if we confess our sins to God, he can always be trusted to
forgive us and take our sins away.
(*Contemporary English Version*)

Confession is good for the soul, isn't it, but when you are little, it just seems too scary to contemplate.

My sister, Stephanie, had a doll. Grandma Gladys had sent it over from England to India as a present. It was beautiful – a real grown-up doll with eyes that opened and closed, as well as what seemed to me to be real eyelashes. Now I was jealous. I am sure Grandma had sent me a doll too but I obviously didn't feel it was as good as Steph's. I had pleaded with her to let me play with it, but she had sensibly refused. And so, I took it when she wasn't watching, and I am ashamed to say, I pulled those eyelashes out. The rest is a blank to me, but I know that I felt bad for many weeks afterwards.

Probably 30 years later, we were all together, reminiscing about our time in India. The story about the doll came up and Mum revealed that she had hinted to Steph that the rats had probably damaged the doll as she was worried about what Steph would do to me if she knew the truth. The image of the damaged doll filled my mind and I remembered the awful thing I had done. Steph thankfully saw the funny side and I was forgiven.

Sometimes we have to laugh at things in our past, and some things are a lot easier to laugh at than others. Shame from our past can cripple us from moving forwards into the rest of our lives but the good news is that when we confess to God, we needn't fear any kind of retaliation, we are met by his grace, not his anger. His forgiveness is free and overwhelming. Nothing more is needed. Let's let go of shame and guilt and move into the freedom He offers us.

Lord, what relief,
what joy.
When I think of all I have done,
and all you have forgiven.
Shame is silenced
by your unconditional love.
In my mind I see you
beckoning me on,
urging me to let go of the past
and walk forwards
into the light of
your forgiveness.

Undercover gnomes

Proverbs 15:30

A twinkle in the eye means joy in the heart, and good news
makes you feel fit as a fiddle.

(*The Message*)

Garden gnomes are something you either
love or hate. Personally I think some are
quite appealing. One of Mum and Dad's
neighbours had several gnomes in their
front garden and for some strange reason,
Dad thought it would be funny to add
another gnome to their collection without
telling them, and see how long it took
them to notice. He planned to plant quite
a few there.

He bought one in a car boot fair and
crept over to their house late one evening
to place it with the others. I can imagine
him running back home laughing to
himself. Time passed and he heard nothing, either from the neighbours with
the gnomes, or any of the others.

From time to time I would ask and he would laugh and say 'No, not yet.'
After Dad had died, I was chatting with the gnome-owning neighbour when
I realised he still didn't know. I pointed
out the gnome and told him the story.
He was so thrilled to know it was Dad.
We had a good time reminiscing about
Mum and Dad, and laughing about the
undercover gnome.

Let's use our imagination and do
something for someone to make
them smile. The gnome is still in the
neighbour's garden, and I am sure he
still makes them smile. I like to think
that God enjoyed the joke too.

Lord, I can take myself too
seriously sometimes,
weighed down by
a long 'to-do' list,
and that in itself can be a
pressure, trying to get things
done, always on the go.
Help me to relax a little,
see the funny side of life
and give me the opportunity to
make someone smile today.